TONGULISH

Rita Ann Higgins was born in 1955 in Galway, where she still lives. She left school at 14, and was in her late 20s when she started writing poetry. She has since published ten books of poetry, including *Sunny Side Plucked* (Poetry Book Society Recommendation) (1996), *An Awful Racket* (2001), *Throw in the Vowels: New & Selected Poems* (2005), *Ireland Is Changing Mother* (2011) and *Tongulish* (2016) from Bloodaxe, and *Hurting God: Prose & Poems* (2010) from Salmon Poetry. *Throw in the Vowels* was reissued in 2010 with an audio CD of her reading her poems. Her plays include *Face Licker Come Home* (1991), *God of the Hatch Man* (1992), *Colie Lally Doesn't Live in a Bucket* (1993), *Down All the Roundabouts* (1999), *The Plastic Bag* (2008), *The Empty Frame* (2008) and *The Colossal Longing of Julie Connors* (2014). Her many awards include a Peadar O'Donnell Award in 1989 and several Arts Council bursaries, and she is a member of Aosdána.

Rita Ann Higgins

TONGULISH

BLOODAXE BOOKS

ISBN: 978 1 78037 303 4

First published 2016 by
Bloodaxe Books Ltd,
Eastburn,
South Park,
Hexham,
Northumberland NE46 1BS.

www.bloodaxebooks.com
For further information about Bloodaxe titles
please visit our website or write to
the above address for a catalogue.

Supported using public funding by
ARTS COUNCIL
ENGLAND

Cover design: Neil Astley & Pamela Robertson-Pearce.

Printed in Great Britain by Bell & Bain Limited, Glasgow, Scotland, on
acid-free paper sourced from mills with FSC chain of custody certification.

For the twins Cooper & Axel Higgins Ryan
born 13th November 2015

For my nephew John Diviney
died 28th or 29th June 2012

CONTENTS

Easy on the Ankle

It was a non-fatal attack
but if that high heel
had gone an inch
one way or the other
he was Long-John-Silvered
without a spoon in his mouth.
He'd have ended up sucking
his porridge through a jackdaw.

And what would he do then –
blame the council I suppose!
'Council assistant takes high heel
to man over parking fine.'

As it was, his eye was hanging out
by its socket.
So much so that he squealed,
half wildebeest, half agony aunt.
People didn't know whether
to laugh or laugh louder,
he was making a right fool of himself.

Anything babe, you can have anything,
even my maggot collection.
And you know the way I am
about them maggots.
You can sell my python on eBay.
Just get help, I'm begging you.

Put a sock in it, she said,
in a guerrilla-warfare voice.
Now hop along for yourself
and think twice before you start
telling me how useless I am.
Capisce!

I'm good for something
as we both can see.
Furthermore, a council assistant
would never wear high heels in City Hall.
They wear flats for comfort,
easy on the ankle,
easy on the eye.

The Waiter

The waiter was flipflopping
all over the place,
flailing in his long fishnet sleeves.
Enough net to catch a dogfish
and a county in.

Menus were flying,
left right, left wrong.
Then up into an arc
and he catches them
on their way home.
They were wine menus.
It was ten a.m.

I was about to ask for coffee.
He sped back to the cutlery station
which looked like a stainless steel grotto.
All knives pointing skywards

He stole a quick look at his reflection
in a chipped dinner plate.
It gave him a kind of three dimensional swag.
His hair looked longer
and thicker, good for a ponytail.

I said just coffee, black.
Wearing my happy Christmas,
I didn't see your reflection
in the plate look.

The indignity of it for him,
and he all menu-draped and driven.
Flailing and pirouetting
thinking brandy-roasted lobster
and pan-seared breast
of Mullingar mallard.

Just coffee, I said again.
He turned in on the baubles
on the lopsided tree.
After a silent scream of
'she only wants coffee'
he started talking in bauble,
and there he lost me.

Now he's on a skateboard
flying past my table.
He did an about-face,
and landed the coffee near me,
four tables down to be precise,
reachable by gannet stretch
or dogged determination.

As I was leaving
he started with the bauble lingo,
rising and falling,
tinsel between his teeth.
He checked me out on the cracked plate,
starting at my heels and working up.
He brayed in bauble and babble
then he lost me,
all over again.

The Middle Man

In a bar in Mayo
two old men sit stools apart
at half eleven
of an August morning.

They will speak to each other
or to the space between
when the time is right.
A slow half-hour might crawl by.

It's changeable, one said.
Very, said the other
after a well-thought-out pause
with a 'Huh' in front of it
that came out like a jibe.

There was a fierce downpour earlier
when I was leaving home.

What direction did you come from?

Another slow moon orbits.

From over beyond.

I see, said the other man
who felt cheated
with no field or furrow
to pinpoint lineage
or at the very least
throw up a surname
that might nail the birthplace,
town, village, or lean-to
of the other soul at the counter.

There's a nice draught from that door,
Downpour said.

I feel nothing. My back is like
the side of a ditch.
I'd block a hurricane, they tell me.
Pity some young wan
wouldn't notice.

Before Downpour could reply,
or crack a half-smile,
a third man came in.

He sat betwixt and between,
making smithereens of their
newly built bridge.
With his *Sun* newspaper
and his mobile phone.

No third man was ever needed
to harness that emptiness
that spilled over
into clipped conversation.
Where staring out and guessing
was the only glue needed,
to weave and stitch
that barren road to no-town
that had nothing much
going for it anyway.

Not even a few potholes
to rattle your insides
and create a chattering sound,
more jabber than jibe
that you reckoned meant something
but really meant nothing at all.

No End to the Amulets

The traveller woman
would pin some holy badge
on the child's pram.
Herself and my mother
catching up on the new arrivals,
or what child had tonsillitis,
or who had the mumps.
All class of saints' names were drawn down:
Frances, Agnes, Saint Gabriel,
Catherine of Siena, Martha, Saint Clare,
Saint Theresa of the Little Flower.

Goodbye was a long way off.
At the mere thought of it
the holy exchange would happen all over again,
more bountiful than before.
One would give
and the other would give more.
No end to the amulets.

A small crucifix for you,
a pair of scapulars for your twins,
holy water from Lourdes,
a few more medals.
Talk of a sick aunt
brought a relic out
from inside her shawl.

The rosy-faced child a beamer,
the Silver Cross pram a shrine.
This side of Mount Sinai
no demon was safe,
Beelzebub, Balaam or Bile.

Getting Older

(for Marion Moynihan)

In Mijas
we climb a little,
we get tired,
we climb some more,
we get tireder,
we turn back.

Two coffees,
and a scoop
of the bull's blood
for me.

On the bus
everyone talks about
the ancient church
at the top of the hill.

We saw nothing
but the randy dogs,
a few orange trees,
a donkey derby.

Costa Del Dento

There he is
eatin' like a horse
with his neck-brace
around his elbow –
robbin' pears from the next table.

He's on the dole at home
with a claim in
against the Corpo
for a dodgy kerb job
only he called it
an f'ing footpath.

You'd have to be on LSD
for your foot to land
on that slanted footpath.
More like gliding
on the rim of a chipped bath.

Here on the Costa
he's making the girls laugh
telling them Errol Flynn
had nothing on him –
and the swelling
only goes down
with gentle kissing.

Any barbarism in him
was well earned
in the Christian Brothers
where they kissed him
nightly with their batons
and he only a child
that still believed in Santa
and the tooth fairy.

The very Christian Brothers
kept knocking his milk teeth out
because of the no word.

They didn't like the sound of no,
so they kicked him again,
and another tooth would orbit
far above his innocence
and land like a sixpence
on a well-polished floor.

DiMaggio Style

In Fuengirola
the pubs
have a throbbing beat
until six a.m.

Then an eerie silence until seven
when the dog walkers
pound the pavement.

Lycra and kool runners,
peaked caps
Joe DiMaggio style.

The dogs have
perfect teeth.
The owners
have 'driven'
written all over them.
Their curlew lipstick,
their crimplene hair.

Mr Grave Offence

No one can hate like a good Christian.

PATSY McGARRY,
Pat Kenny Show, RTE Radio, 8 December 2011

Mr Grave Offence
took a fence, took an inch,
took a crooked mile.
He croaked out
that hurt was only his.
Hurt is only mine, ye swine,
came the chorus.

He had high hopes
for the witch's tongue,
it was loose for too long.
He didn't want to gloss over,
he wanted ectomy, ectomy,
a trophy with a last vowel,
a viper verb,
a sliding to Gethsemane.

Waiting in the wings
with a yard of isolation
were the 'follow the money mob',
rent a mewling crowd of maggots,
rent a crowd of mewling maggots,
same same, me love you long time, money man.

They were all present
except the Unmentionable.
Leave her in the wilderness
came the chorus,
let's hope the dingoes come
and eat her tongue,
it's been loose for too long.

Find her rhyme then
crown her vowel.
Toss her nothing
not even the odd nettle
to soothe her aching eyes.

Shades of Truth

(for RMCC)

> Better to sleep with a sober cannibal than a drunk Christian.
> HERMAN MELVILLE

I might write a poem today,
a watertight poem
where words may dovetail
or even do a handstand.
It could have people in it
or the dead fox
I saw on the way to Costello Lodge,
or the man and donkey
I saw on the way back.
It could have miles of sea and seagulls in it,
Galway seagulls,
unfussy, they go straight for the jugular.
It could have a tablecloth
from the White Star Line in it.

It could have Nantucket in it.
It could have The Spouter Inn in it.
It could have Ishmael and Queequeg
wrapped twice around each other
in a bed made from whale bone and sweat.

If I add the sailor and harpooner
locked in a loving embrace
all the pitch long night
with the harpooner's breath
hot on Ishmael's ear.

It will be different then,
the whole tale will be damned,
tossed asunder
in maelstrom, skylark and yaw.

At Sea

(after Herman Melville)

All the talk of Tashtego and what sperm
he could get for you, my captain.
More praise for his dexterity –
he must have been in a circus
and walked a tight rope.
He walks a fine line here
and he can fairly bend.

Proper show-off,
he never stops essing and hooking,
he barely hides his own tackle,
no shame at all.
Off down with him a bucket attached to his line.
Oh, he won't come up without sperm,
and he'll duck and dive again
for the good stuff, my captain.
He'll never wipe the sweat
so that when he bobs
you'll know how he strives for you –
even with the great one banging at the hull.

With all his posing he slipped and fell,
head first into the hot gurgling spermaceti.
One naked cannibal, my loving Queequeg
dived in, his big sword erect.
He will not come up without that show-off,
dead or alive he'll have him by the hair.
No worries there, my captain.

Thing is, I would have gone in,
lowly sailor that I am.
But with a barrel, not a bucket
and a sawn-off harpoon
between my teeth.

I would have delivered
all five hundred barrels
and never spilled a drop,
and if I did spill it
I would dive again
and drink it before
I'd waste it to the deep.
All for you, *oh Ahab my captain!*

I had no chance with that blowbag Tash –
always wanting the limelight.
Queequeg pulled him out
all covered in sperm,
hot and honeyed, scented even.
Some sailors, who had been out too long,
wanted to reach out to him on his way up,
but fearing ridicule, they did not.

We were all at sea.
We didn't need Sirens to lead us astray.
Some of us were lost,
some of us were longing,
all that sperm long day.

(Spermaceti is created in the spermaceti organ inside the whale's head.)

The Gathering

Most people don't give a shit about the diaspora [in Ireland] except to shake them down for a few quid.

GABRIEL BYRNE,
The Irish Times (10 November 2012)

Our Solomon's stretch on the hill of Tara
with goat horns and megaphones,
coaxing the global diaspora back
to the crossroads for a few crumbs
under the guise of 'The Gathering'.
They rollcall the lost generation
of school leavers and factory workers,
turkey pluckers, thinkers, stinkers,
runaway nuns and qualified nurses.

Bring them all home,
close the fence, don't use corral nouns
or words ending in loose change.
Think millions, think mint.
No need for dead bolts or padlocks
but wrench fence might be advisable.
A quick census and see how the numbers multiply,
throw in a parable or two,
watch out for second-thoughters,
they could try to burrow their way out
of any bango-quango,
much less a closed ward or a ghost estate.

We were seasonally adjusted then
now we are globally adjusted twice over,
still waiting for crumbs at the crossroads.

Our sons and daughters
are coming home.
There are no jobs
only Sallies and Rods,

no Jimmying that one can see,
but the pluckers still pluck
harp, bicycle wheel, or steel comb.

Here austerity is a road sign going nowhere.
Here we have sourdough for monopoly money
with a trifling of psychic scar.
With this global homecoming
we'll have caviar in the jar.

This is a government initiative,
they are calling it 'The Gathering'.
What will really happen is
we'll end up eating grass
while prancing and Riverdancing.
We'll dress in green jerseys
and play the fools,
we'll crack the whip,
we'll take skelps off our own backbones.

Sinner

I'll start again,
I'll come in quietly
with my rosary.
I'll kneel on your footstool
and start my incantation.

I'll start again,
I'll come in quietly
I'll blow out all the candles but one.
I'll kneel on your footstool
and take out my rosary.

This isn't working, I'll start again.
I'll be nimble-footed Athena,
I'll spin that footstool into infinity.
I'll divide my time between the folds
of your holy robes, my liege,
exposing the red satin lining.

Then you sprout indulgences.
No more footstools, my soul wiped clean,
a seat in heaven with the angels.
(Mind you, you did say if I got to hell
it would be out of your hands.)

If only you could be more like
your uncle Callixtus, all penance and prayer.
Alas, you're more like the scoundrel you are,
all devil-tail and dance.

You stretch back and spread your
Pythagorean thighs.
Me, a ghoul for the old indulgence.
I'll blow your anvil for as long as you can stand,
and when you explode
I'll say nothing.

Caligula

You've had all my handmaids.
You think they don't tell me,
they tell me everything.
You forget about Mnemosyne,
she clocks up all your putrid deeds.

Now you sprawl there
with that wine goblet in your hand,
your red lips,
you look more like me than me.
Will you drink it or throw it?
Madness in your eyes –

I know some depraved stuff
is cooking, the eyes never lie.
Before this you were never
bothered much with Cuntus –
a rear-ender, like the rest.

You look at the grapes
and you mad-eye me,
all in the one sycophantic blink.
You fiddle with my toga
using that emperor toe.
Your aim is good
for one so riddled with venom.

Why can't you be more like Benedict
who warded off lust
against his holy sister Scholastica
by rolling around naked
in nettles and thorns?

Emperor of evil
with chiffon sanity.

You boast to the menfolk
our private deeds, Beelzebub.
If I pop those grapes
you'll dunk your nut.
As if Cuntus was vile
and a favour bestowed.
You forget about Mnemosyne
she forgets nothing.
She'll turn you into a horny toad,
or a double take, or better still,
a lost look.

My Claudius

I've been whipped
all the way to oblivion.
You may as well
have stuck me
on that Promethean rock
with endless ocean views
and have my guts plucked daily
by some eager eagle
with bad eyesight
and a penchant for lady liver.

It's too late to say,
touch me not –
when you have touched me
in so many subtle ways, my Claudius.
Your aphrodisiacal rage
always centre-stage.
I'm not just talking about
Pliny the Elder lamping you,
kicking the spite
out of that killer whale
below in Ostia harbour.
More mundane rages move me
to uncontrollable lust.
I had such capital plans.

How often I took down
the golden bull's horn pestle
to mix a love potion.
A touch of mandrake root
to make you hard,
a touch of sowbread
to make you harder.
How often I've had you on your knees?
Cat o' nines on Sun's day
radish root on Moon's day –

Then out of the ether
the crumbs stopped coming –
and so did I.
My empty mouth won't grovel
for the acerbic morsel.
I won't weasel either.
I don't give good weasel.

I might curse you
in my subconscious
and send an eagle of my own,
only, and mark this
my clever Dick, maker of roads,
many's the short cut
you took through me.
No liver seeker am I,
only hoatum-scrotum
one man in an upturned boatum
all the way to Hades
with a shrew in each eye.

But in the wakening,
fighting back no tears
I will let you know,
my Emperor, my cousin,
I know about your womanising.
I know, too, you've given me
the stiff upper
heave-fucking
ho ho ho.

Tongulish

The longest day
of the year has passed.
It sped like Pythia in a chariot
filled with buckshee syllables –
yours for the taking.

Now there will be less time
for you to say more
and you have been known
to speak in tongues
but not lately, Doteling.

I can take any old blather
and you can give it,
but that aching silence
that never satisfies any gulf
is the silence I've come to loathe.

Throw out all full stops,
let your verbs be brazen
but never irregular.
Salute tongue in all its guises,
let Tongulish hop on the bandwagon.
Abbreviate, too, our playful words
not yet invented,
in gibberish, cant, or slang.

Give me garbled, slurred, rasp,
a fricative on its own
or leaning on a noun.
I'll take metaphor, babble,
weight-watcher words with no taste,
jejune compounds, or con words,
whisper, puggle, click or clack words.

Just speak or hold forever,
weasel or wicked words,
worm words, that are worthless,
cutting-down to size words,
that matter, that don't matter.

An Octave Higher

Sometimes you take me
by surprise,
but nearly always
from behind.
You don't even take off that armour
when you take me, lover!
The incantation
from the racket is deafening,
but it's not without
a curious comfort,
an ancient lullaby,
calamitous fuck.

And Jove knows it's heavy.
As heavy as our sins –
and we do sin often
of an afternoon.
Oh Emperor of darkness!
Oh cunning fuck!
Toss me with your Herculean strength
that I might glimpse your vacuous eyes.

Your sandals drenched again –
no doubt you were flailing about
in the Tiber, taking down
a few Christians for *spraoi*
on your way to take me, Godling!
What gets into you?

When you bite my nape
with such gusto
(after me soaking for hours
in asses' milk),
I snap momentarily,
more from startle
than from sting.

When I shudder
from the draught in the vestibule
(if we ever reach the bedchamber
it will be a miracle),
you think it's because of you –
egomaniac,
and you plunge deeper.
I snap again
an octave higher
I say BASTA, Nero, BASTA!
You never listen.

Cutting Edge

In Voltpoint Prison,
seven sets of red secateurs
in perfect nick hang proudly
in a glass case.

On gardening days
they are brought out
and laid on a table.
When you want a pair
you sign for them.

To cut out
wisecrack monikers
like Jack the Ripper,
Gully Guts,
or Vein Villain,
initials will do.

The inmates pull weeds
with their bare hands.
No need for
the dandelion digger here.
For the shrubs
or the conifer branches
they use the secateurs.

A spring
causes the jaws to open.
No motive required,
just aim and bingo
the head of a dying rose
hits the dirt.
The better the secateurs,
the cleaner the cut.

The parrot-beak
is best for the wooded stem
or the contrary knot.
A good secateurs
is for life.

A sign says:
walk gently on the grass.
The inmates, now feather-footed
ballerinas, glide to their cells
hardly touching a blade.

The One with the Sky in His Eyes

A sneer, a mock,
a joke that fell flat,
from the headmaster
with the freckled face.

I'd mimic his wry smile
in a monkey-see monkey-do way.
A sneer that looked
as if a door had closed on it
and brought that *straois* down
to inkwell level.

Where is your brother today?
Is he not well?
I was in first or second class,
old enough to have taken the host,
but not yet a soldier of Christ.

Which one do you mean,
I have hundreds of brothers?
Is it the map reader,
is it the one who could talk to birds,
is it the one with the sky in his eyes?
He's gone to the dispensary
with the prescription
for my mother.

What colour bottle
will he bring back today?
Is today a green bottle day,
or a blue bottle day?

Odd the way the headmaster
changed his voice,
when the mocking started
a ladder up to shriek,

bordering on owl,
brinking on hallelujah.
A sneer for the green bottle day,
or the blue bottle day.
The *straois* now flapping
like a broken umbrella
on a runway.

The stolen canes story
came to mind,
how they were found hidden
in a nearby forge,
under a dirty green canvas.

The impulse was
to strike the headmaster
across the teeth
with the stolen canes.
I divided the strikes
into a long half a hole
in a half a day sum.

If I gave the headmaster
one strike for himself,
one and a half strikes
for every mention
of a green bottle day,
two and a third strikes
for every mention
of a blue bottle day,
a close shave strike
to take that *straois* off his face,
plus one strike for every freckle.

How many strikes
would I have given,
how many strikes
would he have received?

I day-dreamed the answer,
it ran into double figures
dressed in pitch,
cross-eyed with rage.
I drew from an ancient place
or maybe it was only from
a shadow in the hedge
that sang the sibling song.
I drew in a negative gasp
the length and breath
of my scrawny self.
I drew out
a perfect red bottle day.

A Field Day

(for Sarah Clancy)

I love a nice hotel.
I always take a face cloth.
When I go home
I put the face cloth
over my face in the bath.

I rarely think about
the Zabbaleen
in the slums of Cairo.
They work the dumps
sifting with a deft movement.
Bone here, metal here,
cloth and plastic over there.
Any food they find,
they feed it to the pigs first.

The flies swarm
making a massive halo.
The Zabbaleen sift on,
bone here, metal over there.
Soon there will be changes,
big companies will
clean up.

I put in more hot water.
I love a nice hotel.
I always take a face cloth.
When I go home
etcetera etcetera.

When they protest,
they will be washed clean
with the water cannon –
when the Zabbaleen fall back,

the flies will have a field day.

Mirage

At least she had the egg money,
and no one was going to get
their paws on that.
She would not have been so hard
if he had spilled
a thimbleful of nice
in her direction ever.
But no, from day one
the toughness was there.
His dry lips frightened her,
she knew that he had
not spoken to anyone
for hours, maybe days.

Now it was her turn
to hear the barb of his roll-call.
Off he went down Resentment Drive
and he let her have it
about how sorry he was
the day he ever laid eyes
on this no-good-good-for-nothing,
who couldn't even
boil an egg.

And if she heard it
often enough, and she did,
she began to believe it
and it made her smaller.
Her shrinkage
was slow to start
but in the end
she felt like,
a speck of dirt
a flick of ash
or something in front
of the eye.

Cavity

I saw myself
before I got shingles.
My chakras aligned
all the way to Pluto.
An indigo aura
in my salsa jeans.
A flirt with a few teeth missing.

Crusoe

I was sitting
in my car at Ballyloughane beach.
Stinging stinging.
I saw a cruise liner in the distance.
Joyous sounds,
I could make out dancing.
Salsa and boogie woogie.
I stood on the roof
and shouted out,
'Take my shingles yo,
and plant them in Honolulu.'

Blue Begonias

Are you lonesome,
the man said,
wearing his sliding face,
his eyes covered
in blue begonias.

When you have shingles,
the supreme dose,
they creep in under the nipple
keeping you awake,
the lover you don't love.
They sting and sting.
You'd give anything
for a bit of lonesome.

The Seers

They were looking
and blessing themselves.
I overheard a woolly mammoth say
the TB didn't get her
but the shingles will.
She'd need to make sacrifice
and a monastery won't do.
She'd need to go all out
and beg on her maudlin knees.

Spell

I burned
a corduroy trouser
under a horse's nose.
I let the cure man
blow on me three times.
Once for the sows,
once for the cows
and once for the rottweiler
that lives down the lane.
I put a used tea bag
in a taxi man's pocket
like Tommy Cooper told me.
The next day
the shingles were back
just like that.

The Deed

The marks on my back
are like tiger claws,
shingled out for reference
on the last day.
The song of the crow was clear.
She's going to burn
she did something bad
to a priest
that didn't involve
penance or prayer.

Marked

It's April
and I still have shingles.
They prod me
like Lucifer's fork.
A prick for a sin,
a sting for a prick.
Venial or mortal
no matter.

Pig Iron

Now I'm juicing,
trying to beat the shingles.
Things that don't even rhyme,
turnip and orange
cabbage and kiwi.
The colour is enough
to shrink a liver.

Usually the end result is a drink,
but today I was crushing
something hard,

a child's tooth,
a wedding ring,
the butt of a horseshoe.

The Party

(for Maura Kennedy)

The Dancers
came out of a hole in the wall.
They danced to
Blue Eyes Crying in the Rain.
Women had bright clothes on,
a splash of gingham,
a spray of cerise.
Yellow umbrellas
were all the raging.
So were little rat dogs,
they danced too, kind of.
They were leashed around,
swinging on the bends of chairs.

A man shadow danced
on his fingertips.
His nails worn down.
He had fences on his teeth.
Not the type you'd jump
but the type you'd jump over
to kiss them, mossy green and whites.
I was seeing them
upside down –
so don't get me wrong.

He whistled out
...in the rain...
and my hair went all woof woof,
and I was la la lawing –
to the two-man band.
Then he said, all wide-eyed,
remember the buckle factory.
I'm heading in your direction, honey –
keep your sacred heart light burning.
Keep your side gate a-swing.

Morsus

On the morning
my father died
the fridge
was so empty
you could hear

a crumb drop.

Glimpse

I'll come back as a hare
and race the-ins-and-outs of Letterfrack.
I'll run rings around the dark place
and flit past memories that might hurt a hare.
I'll be half seen by the Letterfrackers
in the semi-darkness that draws a limping shadow.
'I thought I saw a hare today standing on his hind legs
looking in the pub door.'

One day a blackbird called my name,
it sang out as I raced the loop of Letterfrack.
I wanted to stop then and take a well-earned rest.
My ears up for any ancient sound, a whisper or a howl.
It was a scratch that came, my throat aflame,
a female voice, more urgent than I'd known.
She said, Salute the blackbird and the lark,
give the crow a wide berth, side-eye him only.
He carries a lucky bag of omens, unlucky for some.
Never chase the cry of the weasel
or you'll end up in no town, lost and lonely.
Run my son and never stop.

Chaste

Your whip tongue
a bull's eye.
I limp away.

Later you slip
a threepenny bit
under my pillow.

I open one bruised heart.

The Odd Wasp

I have seen women who were ashen
with venial sin and hardly able to stand
with the thrashing they got
from the holy spirit.
They had faint hope that some day
life was going to be easier.
Faint hope is better than no praise at all.
In the catacomb of their
what-da-ya-ma-call-it
there was a drinker to be prayed for,
everyone had one of them gigglers.

There was the child whose name was Donal,
everyone called him special.
A gentle child with no malice.
He played ball against the side of a house,
a different house every day.
Bong bong bong, with a hard red ball.

It was reckoned
that if Donal died in his sleep
he'd go straight to hell
because he had not taken some sacrament
that gave him a bypass-hell voucher.

Other moral deficiencies were figured
on a sliding scale of the indignant adult
whose nose was in the next county
making several about-face-chin-jerks a week
about the weight of sin
a few arraghs thrown in.

People at the centre of things
couldn't cope with nice and gentle
and no trace of malice.

That's why special laid nicely
across the young lad's brow.
Ahhh always came before a wall,
ahhh came before a lot of things
and God help us was never far behind.
Donal didn't come from a hive of copers.
Neither did the women who were ashen
with venial sin.
They came from a hive of
ahhh-ers and blamers.
They ahhhed the day away
talking casually of the no-harm
that was inbuilt in all of us.

Out of that hive came the odd wasp.
One such wasp was christened
Thomas Mary-Aquinas Legume,
known locally as Tommy-the-Hammer.
He picked up his nickname
not by chance or any hidden elegance
but by an evil force that made him do it.
At the communal well people said,
about Tommy the H: Ahhh the poor devil;
and the second row said:
ahhh God help us.

Primula Vulgaris

In May the statue of Our Lady
was cleaned and put out
in a sheltered place in the garden.
A lick of blue paint took years off her,
we dolled her up further with bouquets of mayflowers.
We'd put a string of primroses around her neck
and another one above the front door.
The fairies would never pass
over or under a primrose string.

Yesterday when I was leaving Annegret's
for a walk down to the shore,
the primroses were out to play.
As I walked they seemed to walk.
Some decked a hedgerow,
other clusters claimed a field.
How could they be *vulgaris* anything?

We'd put fresh flowers
around Our Lady's statue.
She was a good protector
against the dark forces.
We had to be on our guard,
our side eye never closed.
Demons hid under every cowslip.

As for the fairies,
they had no dark side,
only mischief makers in the main.
They might toss a bucket in the air
or move a spade that was left against a wall.
Or so we thought. Did you see that spade move?
Who tossed that bucket in the air?
'Puck did' was the only reply.

On my way back to the house
the primroses were there again,
more plentiful than before.
Who sprayed that hill?
Who knitted that hedgerow?
I walk through a funnel of colour,
a pale yellow dress,
not a fairy in sight.
Sabhaircín sabhaircín.

Audition

In Na hAille
the clouds
are nearly reaching
the tips of the trees.
I can hardly see
the sea.
Luckily for me
not every conifer takes –
there is a gap.
I gape through it
from where I sit
at Annegret's table.

I see Lisa passing
in her silver car.
She waves,
I wave back.

I might write a poem today –
if only something
would come to me.
Then again there's always
daytime TV.

I wonder if Lisa
knows anything
about the londubh
who calls me out
in this weather.
Singing like it was an audition
for Carnegie Hall.

I wonder where Lisa goes
in her silver lining.

Testimony

Mother Ireland – get off our backs.

MAIRÉAD FARRELL

The search behind icons
found women in sepia
with frills and flounces,
pursed lips, tightly closed
angelic, divine.
Oh my dark Rosaleen,
you make me sick to my spleen
with your icons and figments,
my sisters you demean.

The silver poets
had silver tongues,
they could make fools
and figments out of anyone.
On the other hand
there was an old woman
who lived in a field,
her name was Ireland
she didn't know who to shield.

The territory
a hinterland of scars,
a pinched nerve
stretching the sinews
won't call a halt
to the voice from the shadows
'If you're Irish throw down your nation.'

The nation that was never once again.
It was mostly once again lost,
twice again displaced,
thrice you're an interloper.

The country that turned on its high heel,
like the insulted relative at a christening,
where someone named the child Perpetua.
The moon tried its saucery,
the tide brought you back again,
or was it the lingo, was it the loss?

Away from motif and memory
some good, some treacherous,
there was always the other hand.
Not the one that rocked the cradle,
not the one that lost the green field,
the other one.

On the other hand
and with no yowling
or head shaking
or body swaying,
women were poeming
not with aislings or needles
but with tongue.
A tongue to rhyme with,
a tongue to lullaby,
a tongue to make history.

Bingham

Bingham was bucking
about that brazen bitch
going over to England
to chinwag with the Queen.
He started a blistering blog
to Sir Morrow What,
saying if that cailleach
says anything about him
it's a pack of dead flies.
She is nothing but
a pirate upstart
who uses men as sex objects.
She has been known to make jokes
about cock size.
She would plunder the eye
out of your skull, polish it up
and wear it round her neck.
Don't give her anything like oxygen.
No sustenance of any kind.
She can live off little.
So my advice to you,
Sir Morrow What,
is give her less than little,
and give her less than little, a lot.

The Visit

Grace was not barefoot,
but she was barefaced
when it came to
ratting on Bingham.
After all, on his wagging tongue
he had her son arrested
and her brother thrown in jail
in two halves.
The Queen said,
Leave it with me, Gracie,
your son and your half-brother
are free from the moment
this blog gets back to Bingham.
Bellicose Bingham won't cross me
and if he does,
I'll embroider his lips together.
He's too free with that tongue anyway
that long lizard lolly.
As you say yourself,
if he had half as much between his legs.

The Reply

The blog Queen Elizabeth
sent him was bleeding
from the knuckles.
Bingham nearly burst
a giblet with the dressing-down
she gave him:

'Leave the queen of Connacht alone
or I'll have your arms.
Let her half-brother
Dónal-na-Piopa out of prison
or I'll have your legs.
Let her son Tibbot-na-Long
go, and stop stalking him,
or I'll have your life
miserable as it is.

Are you listening to me, Bing?
I could take a lift down the Thames
from the O'Malley galley
and spread your insides on a rock to dry.
Mind you, the same galley
wouldn't have cosy enough
for half my embroidered frocks.

So read this
and chew it slowly.
Or I will have You chewed
and spat out on the same rock
as your entrails.

Don't have me
go as far as ya, Bing.
Listen to me now,
there's a good governor.

Cryanair

The queue was long.
The chatter rising up and down
the length of it was anxious,
especially from the elderly.
Some Cryanair soldier
is striking fear into the hearts
of the passengers in Liverpool airport.
It was about carry-on luggage.
I wasn't too worried, my bag was small.
I had used it several times before.

The chief Crier
was walking up and down the queue
saying in a loud voice.
You have three choices
if your bag does not fit in exhibit A,
(pointing to the grill for measuring misery),
one, you pay seventy euros cash,
two, you pay seventy euros by credit card,
or three, you leave your bag.
Ist das klar?

I have to rule out credit card
as I had a problem with mine before I left home.
None of this will apply to me anyway.
I was only there for two days,
how much money was I going to need?
My small bag, my nifty bag.
It will fit like toast.

It didn't, the wheels stuck out.
Juggle things a woman said,
rearrange things in the bag,
it's a tiny bag. Stick your high heels
in the side pockets and try again.
The wheels still stuck out.

The Crier was a Cryanair soldier,
and he was taking no prisoners.
You have three choices he said, over and over.
We knew his choices by heart,
we didn't need to hear them again.
I asked him if his mother knew
how he was treating people.
Don't go down that road with me, lady.
Just pay the money or leave the bag.

I got this Liverpool jersey for my grandson,
it took all my spare cash.
I'm a Cryanair soldier, lady.
We don't do Mother Theresa crap.
Pay the money or leave the bag.

Can I speak to the manager, please?

I'm the only manager
you need to please.
You have three choices he said,
clicking his teeth:
You can pay the seventy euros cash,
you can pay the seventy euros by credit card,
or you can leave the bag.
He counted me down in minutes:
you have twelve minutes,
you have eight minutes,
you have five minutes,
you have no minutes.
The Crier won.
I went down on my hands and knees
and collected my belongings.
I stuffed them into a nylon bag
that I bought for a dollar in Canada months before.
It had Winners written on it.
I left my nifty bag
with the buck wheels at the boarding gate.

I felt like the biggest loser
walking across the tarmac.
Small items falling out the corner hole
of my Winners bag.
I looked back at the toothpaste,
my travel-size bottle of Argan oil
to nail down my wiry hair.
A pair of pink knickers
forty years too young for me.
I saw the Crier
a lean and mean figure
inside the glass, just looking.
A new queue was forming.
There was misery to measure
and he was hand-picked to do it.
He turned on his heel.

I'd swear I heard a click.

I'll Give Good Plinth

Each one must give as he has decided in his heart,
not reluctantly or under compulsion,
for God loves a cheerful giver.

CORINTHIANS 9:7

Will I give back the 70K severance pay?
I'll make a statement later today.
I won't take the hump
but I might take the lump.

I'll tell you all later
from the plinth at Leinster House
and everyone will be watching
and I will be taller.
And my right hand will know
what my left hand is doing.
Have your cameras ready,
snap me as I have snapped you.
I am a giver everyone knows that.
I will stand on the plinth at Leinster House
and give and give till my eyes bleed.
Shy retiring person that I am.
I hate publicity
but on this occasion
I will make a plinth exception.
I'll wear my platform shoes.
A few inches taller
is a few inches taller.
No, I won't answer on national radio
early in the morning what I'm
going to do with the money, honey.
I'll wait for me as you all have waited for me.
I'll take a deep breath.
I'll have someone wipe the sweat from my tie,
I'll low and I'll hold and I'll give good plinth.

While the Earworm Fiddled

It was no harm
getting the odd clatter
that would make your earring
a liberty bell.
The odd kick,
that folded you over
like Sancho Panza's ass,
was harder to take.

A stone wall of negatives
weaved its way in –
an earworm fiddling with your balance.
The negatives were Irish words for fool:
amadán, óinseach, pleidhce, leibide.
Most times you could shrug them off,
leave fool words on the road
to get run over by a trucker
on the way to the maternity
to see his new twins.
You could juggle fool words
above your head and flick them
to infinity or further.

Except some nights
when you were caught
in that gap that was half way
in and out of sleep,
when the long wall of negatives
rocked up and roll-called you
every Irish word for fool.
It was then and only then
that you knew for sure
the damage was done.

The Search

> And when I looked at you
> I missed myself.
>
> ELENA SHVARTS (1948-2010)

I was looking for a different book altogether.
A friend had asked if I had *Breakfast with Mao*.
It was on my bookshelf for years,
now I couldn't see its yellow cover anywhere.

I plucked out *Paradise* by Elena Shvarts.
Seeing her book brought it back to me:
that meeting with her,
the night of her Cúirt reading,
Brennan's Yard Hotel,
a place for the afterburners.
We talked over whiskey one
over whiskey two,
over writers, over mothers,
over fat cats, over birds of pray,
over house birds and Petersburg birds.

She was mostly Winter
but the gentlest winter
that ever fell.
It had lots of pet days.
No need for a thaw,
there was no ice.
Unfixable isolation
was only half-the-picture,
hello despair.
Light was leaning in
maybe not every chance it got,
but certainly it was leaning,
hello honeysuckle.
Knowing there is nothing wrong
with darkness, she hello'ed it.

She kept it mostly on her sleeve.
Snowflakes on her shoulders,
hello light.
A river of sadness can have
the odd Chinese lantern on it.
Just pass in the cigarettes,
hello bliss.

She wrote her name and address
on a paper napkin. We would write,
there was no question about that.
Her eyes confirmed it.

We never did.

Echo

In the dream
my sister was sitting
on a deserted bench
in a long empty room.
Everything was stretched
like in a Dalí painting,
stretched and dripping.

She was on her mobile phone
to my other sister in Piscataway.
I could barely hear
the Piscatawain sister's voice.
It was more like an echo
or an echo's echo.
I thought I heard outside noises
from Piscataway,
like a dog barking.
A dog with no tail or sense,
or a dog's barking echo.

But last I heard her dog had died.
That was a few years ago,
maybe she got another dog.
Maybe it was a neighbour's dog.
After a long convulsive bark
half caught in the echo
half tempered with woe,
it came out as a howl
an echo-ey howl
there was a silence.

I thought I heard a noise.
A crackling, no a breaking.
A heart, whose, mine!
I'll never know.
It was a bad line.
A very bad line.

She's Easy

They're my things, she says,
washing the front step
until it sings,
and cleaning the toilet.
She loved that programme
about the OCDers.
She felt closer to the cleaners
than the counters
or the checkers.
She was a clean fiend once
but she narrowed it down to
front step and toilet.
After that the house could fall down
for all she cared.
When she cleaned she sang,
mostly happy songs.
Elvis and Roy Orbison,
Pretty woman walkin' down the street...
She'd belt out
I found my thrill on Blueberry Hill.
The new water charges bothered her though,
when she thought of the water charges
she couldn't sing.
The room in her head with the tunes
was locked down like Alcatraz.
She says she can't afford to pay
the water charges, simple as that.
I like a bath did I tell you that?
Yeah, I like a bath, and a shower
just before and after I use the toilet.
Apart from that, I'm easy.

Whack

That chair
should be tucked in so far
in the space between
that you'd never notice
a knock knee
or a lean-to-light-bill,
much less a long
afternoon with no coal.

She is tidying up,
putting empty in its place,
threadbare cushions in a row.

The range is cold,
it will be easy to clean.
A wipe down.

She dreams a big fire,
proud and ferocious.
Kids full to their gullets
with exotic food,
bread and ham.

She waits for that time
in her tidy room
in front of the telly,
when ministers bleat
and the budget pounces,
beating her to a pulp.

Guess What

Two wrongs
don't make a right,
the politician said.

OK, we threw billions
at the roads.
We meant to throw it
at the health service.

We did try
and we did throw,
but guess what!
we did miss.

The Carer

You couldn't use the word mental.
You could only say, she wasn't well,
or she isn't herself this weather.
Karen got the carer's allowance,
it was her job to care.
She cared the bejasus out of her mother.

Her mother said that the FBI
were sending her messages
and she was also getting directives from Rome.
Karen used to say to her,
give up that oul talk mammy
or you'll end up in 'the garage'.
Karen was getting tired
of all the lifting, the arse wiping.
The government only paid her a pittance.

Worse than that
Declan was missing
the fuck out of Karen.
Where are you, Karen he'd say,
freezing his tail off on the landing.

It took Karen hours to roll
her mother over
and hours to roll her back.
Karen's days were all rolled into one.
The mother's voices
were going into Karen's head,
they were getting louder.
Karen was having
a little breakdown of her own.
Complete with directives from Rome
and FBI tag-alongs.

The whisper police in the family were off.
No carer of ours is having a breakdown.
There'll be no breakdown on our watch,
only this was her watch.

Declan had the right hump
about the lack of his conjugals.
He pretended it was other things
that pissed him off.
He told Karen to stop her carry-on,
bursting into tears at the breakfast table
and spreading gloom all over the house.
He told her, in a mad man's voice,
to stop collecting those fears
like ornaments from Woolworths.

Fears about the postman bringing bad news,
fears about the angelus bells,
that they were going to fall
from the sky and level us.
He cited twenty-seven other fears
all interlinked and ending in hope
with a no in front of it.

Karen no longer knew what cope meant.
It was a bandied-around word
like biscuit or duty.
Duty got a right outing,
mostly from Declan
whose bulge was going nowhere.
It sat on his lap like a clocking hen.

When Karen's mother slipped
and broke her hip on an ice cube
Karen ran clean out of cope.

Madge

I only knew one Madge
who had no second name.
She took nothing
by any circuitous route
and no man's name
would ever join hers
in bedlock or wedlock.

She was Madge of the wars
and we looked out from behind our
buttoned-up-to-the-neck cardigans
that often had a sacred heart badge
pinned to the gym slip
that kept the cardigan clean.

We knew Madge from the dispensary.
Her goal was to take down the man
from behind the glass,
her mouth full of titanic words.
The rest of us were collectors,
we collected coloured bottles
for a chesty cough,
or drops for a sick eye.
Older women, and they all seemed old,
spoke of colic and measles,
tonsillitis and mumps were always popular.
We never heard of scabies, rabies or dermatitis.

Madge stood in the battlefield
calling him out from behind the glass.
When she stared
it was never into the past
but straight ahead
into a place not yet furrowed
where blame had clout
and standing up for yourself
had its own currency.

She never wore lipstick,
she used war words with accuracy.
That was her own blood
on her dried-asunder lips.
She told him behind the glass
that his own mother
ended up in the poor house
with dirty ankles
because he and his clan
were skirting on the rim of decision
for a half-cup of a century.
Madge never left with any potion
that wasn't already ingested
years ago from hard knock hill.
She tore out sporting a got-ya-fizz,
the belt of her long brown coat
snagging in the door.
The watchers unsure
who the viperous taunts were aimed at.
She kept going apace.
Her lips now bleeding
her tongue never tied
but always spit-firing,
her honour intact.

The Mission

I think of the last time we met
on the prom in Galway.
A sunny day in May
you looked cool in those shades.
You looked taller somehow.
We talked for ages.
You told me about plans
for your mother's sixtieth.
I felt lucky to have such a nephew.
Shades or no shades.

You hid your distress well, John.
None of it was evident that sunny day.
The day of good nephews.
A month later you went to Beachy Head.
WTF John.

I think of you
leaving your bundle
on top of Beachy Head.
Your belt coiled around your watch,
your wallet with a photo of your daughter,
your firefighter's ID card,
your blood donor card,
your bus ticket from Brighton.
Losers weepers.

Margaret, your Irish twin,
was on a holiday she didn't want to go on.
She had been worried sick,
she had us all demented
saying you were going to do it.
Twins know things, Irish twins know more.
I was at a wedding in June
when some friends of yours called me outside.
'It's about John Diviney,'
and something about Beachy Head.

Later we went to the priest,
he came down to Castle Park
to tell your mother.
She thought we were there to show her the wedding style.
I wouldn't mind, John
but I had hired a dress for the wedding.
It was a deep blue.
It sailed when I walked.
Your mother was in a daze.
'I dreamed of him on Thursday night,' she said.
'He went in and out of every room.
Himself and Shannon were laughing.'

We went to Eastbourne to bring you home.
Your mother to collect a son,
Margaret to collect a brother,
Caroline and Majella to collect a cousin.
Me to collect a nephew.
Five women on a mission.

Your mother couldn't sleep,
she was smoking out the hotel window.
She saw the undertaker
collect your best suit from reception at six a.m.

Despite all the sadness
we had laughed a lot on the way over.
The girls nearly missing the flight
because they had to get food.
We laughed, too, at nothing at all.
Declan, another cousin of yours, turned up
and chauffeured us around Eastbourne
and later to Heathrow.
Losers weepers.

You had a photo in your wallet
of your daughter.
I have a photo in my study
of the day we bumped into the two of you
at King's Cross.

Ye were going to some match or other.
What are the chances?
We were over to surprise Heather
on her thirtieth.

What are the chances of bumping into you now, John?
We weren't laughing when we saw you in that coffin.
Your Irish twin ran outside and puked.
Your mother whispered things in your ear.
We started the prayers,
it was a mumbo jumbo litany.
We couldn't remember how anything finished.
Hail Mary, full of grace, the Lord is with thee...

On the way back
there was a bad storm.
We were at the airport for five hours.
Your mother kept going back out for a smoke.
Each time she went out we worried
that she'd never get back in.

You were in the hold,
in your new suit,
your designer shirt,
your best shoes.
We forgot your socks.
Losers weepers.

We arrived at Shannon
in the early hours.
The Divineys were there en masse.
So were Keith and Aidan.
We followed the hearse,
a night cortège.
'At least we have him back,'
your mother said, more than once.

After the funeral mass
your friends from the fire station
hoisted your coffin onto the fire brigade.

The army were there, too.
It was a show stopper.
I never told you this, John,
but I love a man in uniform.

I think of you
leaving your bundle
on top of Beachy Head.
Your belt coiled
around your watch,
your wallet,
with a photo of your daughter,
your firefighter's ID card,
your blood donor card,
your bus ticket from Brighton.
Losers weepers.

'It's about John Diviney,'
the coroner's office said.
'Some young people found his things.
His belt a loop around them.'
He flew without wings
off Beachy Head.
He landed at the bottom,
his back against the wall,
his eyes looking out to sea.

The Bottom Lash

One that is ever kind said yesterday:
My dearest dear,
your temples are starting to resemble
the contents of our ash bucket
on a wet day.

What's with your eyelashes?
They grow more sparse by the tick tock.
Are you biting them off
or having them bitten off,
like the lovers do during intimacy
in the Trobriand Islands?

You have no bottom lashes at all.
Personally, I wouldn't be seen out
without my bottom lash.
A bare bottom lash is tantamount
to social annihilation.

A word to the wise, my dearest dear,
the next time you lamp the hedger
you might ask him to clip clop
your inner and outer nostril hairs.
It's not a good look for a woman.

By the by, doteling,
I've noticed the veins on your neck
are bulging like billio
when a male of the species
walks into the room.
Is that a natural phenomenon?
Or is it a practised technique?
Up or down, you'll get no accolades for it,
nor for the black pillows
under your balding eyes.
Apart from that, my dearest dear,
your beauty is second to none.

The Extra Second

On the last minute
of the last day in June,
we got an extra second.
A leap second, hold that tune.
Oh secunda.

What would you have done
with that extra second?
You might have stretched its neck,
or in a reckless tick you might have
called Madame Blavatsky.
Gyrus, pyrus, tell me. Told.
Where would that second fit
in your leap thinking? Scold.
Oh secunda.

In a hundred years,
second on top of second
would amount to,
one minute and forty seconds –
give or take.
A lot could happen in that expanse,
a lot could happen in your Sunday pants.
You would tell anyone who'd listen
that the earth is slowing down.
But not you, not for one Steinach minute.
You are invigorated
in pituitary, oh secunda.
The sideliners blah blahing
said it was all only a cod.

You'd knock sparks out of that second.
You'd tell them the days are getting longer,
the moon is behind a bush.
Tidal friction is giving
Venus and Jupiter the hump,
but not you, oh secunda.

That second would be melted down
and minted into verb or song.
You'd sit with George.
You, her, table and pen. Bold.
Take that second, George,
spin it first, then let it fly
and see what sentence it will mould.
Oh secunda.

Flight

Her name got lost
in the rush.
They don't give any warning
when they're going to sack
the village.

She just fled.
One child on her hip,
the other two gripping
that cotton dress.

The link was ancient,
unspoken, unwritten.
Their tears were real.
She had nothing
to give them,
only she was theirs
and they were hers.

When she got so far
outside the village
she took a breath,
and looked back.
No salt, no ceremony,
just smoke.
A lot of smoke.

She walked and walked.
The children never let go.
One sob in tandem with the other,
a comforting beat.

They walked for days.
Too exhausted to cry any more
the children were silent.

At night she nods for short spells,
not long enough to be called naps.
Night noises frighten her.
They huddle together,
a fretful sleep.

Another community let them stay.
Now she just wants to stand here
for as long as she walked.
She is Aung San.
She is Teresa.
She is Malala.

If the Shoe Fits

We are waiting for the twins,
about four weeks to go.
You viber me a picture of your swollen foot.
I viber back –
Raise that hoof.
You do what your mother tells you.
Later I'm thinking, what's in the fridge?
She'll be down in the morning starving.
She uses the twins as an excuse for everything.
Can I have a mommy omelette and or
a ham and cheese toasty,
with scallions,
not the other kind of onions
that gives me the pip?
And something nice for afters,
with no 'free from' in it.
She says it's not me it's the twins,
they hate that 'free from' shit.
I say to myself, she's only thirty-five,
give or take.
When she's not munching,
she's crunching ice cubes –
really fuckingannoying.
Annoying in the same the way
some people eat apples,
loud and look at me I'm eating an apple,
or the rare carrot eater, big production job.
I'm thinking about that heavy-looking hoof.
I viber back,
Where the fuck is your other foot?

The Women of 1916

...the state recognises that by her life within the home...

ARTICLE 41.2.1. THE IRISH CONSTITUTION

Years before the offending article
was even conjured up by De Valéra
and the very Reverend John Charles McQuaid
with the help of a pack of Jesuits –
the plan was set in train
to banish these biddies
back to their kitchen sinks.

The banishing tool of choice
was the airbrush.
The women of 1916
did not sit back
and wait in the wings of history
with tricolour dribblers to mop
the runny eggs
from the chins of the rebels.
These Unmanageables
were there from the start.
They could knit
a thirty-two county Ireland
in plain and purl,
with their eyes closed
and never drop a stitch,
while rearing seven sons
and as many daughters.
The rifles they held
were not for showing
but for using.
The handgun could nestle on a hip
or be tucked into a petticoat.
Webley, Colt, Smith and Wesson.

Winnie (with the Webley) Carney
was one of the last people out of the GPO,
revolver in one hand, typewriter in the other.

I write it out in a verse:
Lily O'Brennan, Constance Markievicz,
Helena Moloney, Ellen 'Nellie' Gifford,
May Moore, Rosie Hackett, Dr Kathleen Lynn
Margaret Skinnider, Rose McNamara,
Nell Ryan, Lizzie Mulhall, Kathleen 'Kitty' Fleming...

Whenever green dresses are worn,
some tricolour dribblers spill scorn.

The Camp

A stray kick sends the football
into the toilet area. Lost.
What will the children do now?
The camp is a cough of land
with countless refugees jammed into it. Lost.
If you take a breath, it is not yours,
someone has used it before you.
You own nothing here. Lost.

The wire fence, six metres high,
is for your benefit, the man with the gun says.
The grown-ups murmur to their children
how lucky they are.
Look at Aylan Kurdi, where was his luck?

Where did laughter go?
Where did privacy go?
Where did childhood go?

ACKNOWLEDGEMENTS

Some of these poems or versions of them have previously appeared in the following publications: *Ploughshares*, Spring 2015, ed. Neil Astley; *Birmingham Poetry Review*, No 41 ed. Adam Vines; *Poetry Salzburg Review*, nos 22 & 24 Irish, ed. Caitríona O'Reilly; *The Moth Magazine*, issue 8, Spring 2012, ed. Rebecca O'Connor; *The Yellow Nib*, No 8, ed. Leontia Flynn & Frank Ormsby; *The Irish Times* culture section, 2014, ed. Gerard Smyth, *THE SHOp*, nos 46/47, ed. John & Hilary Wakeman; *Poetry Ireland Review*, issue 116, W.B. Yeats special issue, ed. Vona Groarke.

Rody Gorman translated 'Morsus' to Scots Gaelic for An Guth 2015. The poem 'Mirage' was given with love to The Saol Project as part of their 20th anniversary poetry project, www.saolproject.ie

'Glimpse' was commissioned by Leo Hallissey for the Letterfrack Poetry Trail 2014. 'The Bottom Lash' was commissioned by Vona Groarke for the Yeats Special Issue of *Poetry Ireland Review*, issue 116. 'The Extra Second' was commissioned by *Sunday Miscellany* for a special programme on Yeats recorded in Drumcliff Church on 25 July 2015 and broadcast by RTE Radio 1 on 2 August 2015. 'Flight' was commissioned by Oxfam Ireland for Culture Night 2015 and published in *Make Them Visible: Fifteen Irish Writers Imagine Life as a Refugee.*

'The Camp' was commissioned by the Rona Mathlener Projects Foundation (RMP) in relation to the Netherlands taking over the Presidency of the European Union and organising events during first half of 1916. The poem will be spoken and or shown throughout Amsterdam in early May, and shown at Schipol airport and at the beginning of every cultural event.

Arena with Sean Rocks broadcast a special tribute for the poet's 60th birthday in May 2015, when several of the poems were read. Some of these poems were read on *The Brendan O'Connor Radio Show* on RTE Radio 1 on 16 July 2015. 'Pig Iron' was broadcast on *Playback* on RTE Radio 1 on 18 July 2015. 'The Bottom Lash' was read on *Arena* on Culture Night, 18 September 2015 in Meeting House Square, Dublin, in front of a live audience. 'The Women of 1916' was broadcast on Arena on 14 October 2015.

Thanks to John Walsh, Adrian Frazier for the tickets to Druid Shakespeare, Lisa Frank, Eva & Eoin Bourke, Annegret Walsh, Christy, Heather and Jennifer Higgins, Oisín Ó Maca, age six, for the line 'black pillows under your eyes' in 'The Bottom Lash'; Mikey Gannon, the computer man; Pamela Robertson-Pearce for suggesting the cover image.

Irish words

cailleach: witch
spraoi: fun
straois: sneer
sabhaircín: primrose
londubh: blackbird
amadán, óinseach, pleidhce, leibide: fool.